✤ ✤ ✤ ✤ ✤ ✤ ✤ ✤ ✤ ✤

To: _Bonnie_

From: _Tonia_

✤ ✤ ✤ ✤ ✤ ✤ ✤ ✤ ✤ ✤

Bonnie
Lorrie

Dear Friend...

This is a book to give to an old friend, or a new friend, or someone you would like to be a friend, or someone who simply needs a friend.

Dear Friend...

*what you've always wanted to thank a
friend for but never got around to saying*

Noah benShea

SOURCEBOOKS, INC.®
NAPERVILLE, ILLINOIS

Published by Sourcebooks, Inc.
P.O. Box 4410, Naperville, Illinois 60567-4410
(630) 961-3900
FAX: (630) 961-2168
www.sourcebooks.com

BenShea, Noah.
Dear friend / by Noah BenShea.
p. cm.
ISBN 1-4022-0178-8 (alk. paper)
1. Friendship—Miscellanea. I. Title.
BF575.F66B446 2003
177'.62—dc21
2003008465

Printed and bound in the United States of America
IN 10 9 8 7 6 5 4 3 2 1

This book is dedicated to my friends:
too many to name,
too important to forget.

Dear Friend,

This is a book to give to an old friend, or a new friend, or someone you would like to be a friend, or someone who simply needs a friend. This is also a book we might want to give ourselves to remind us how much we need friends, or what it takes to be a friend, or how much less we would be if we were less even one friend. Let someone know that they matter to you because sometimes in life this is all that matters.

For a while now I have been saying "hello" to people with the greeting, "Hello, my friend." I was first greeted this way by a Mexican gardener who did not know me but extended his friendship on meeting, and it struck me that this was a wonderful way to greet the world—perhaps because life too often does not greet us in friendship.

All of our friends don't look like us, and some when we first met didn't even like us. Friends are like mirrors. Sometimes the only thing worse than a bad mirror is a good one. Good friends aren't always people who agree with us, and often that is what makes good friends great.

I have been blessed with many friends. Some remain as friends. Some have been taken by time. And some who shared my path have now taken different roads. This does not make them less; it does mean I see them less often. And this book is also written for friends at a distance—to remind them of what was then and that we honor who they are now. Friendship gives us that. It gives us permission with others to not need to be right.

All of us have had moments when we've been wronged by friends or have wronged a friend, and this book is also written to say, "I'm sorry" and "I understand." I have often been served by putting these two terms as two coins in my pockets and knowing when to leave which where. None of us are less for knowing when we have been less. All of us are more when we are more understanding. And friendship surely understands this.

Life is short and the world cold, and sometimes the best way to get warm is to hug someone else. We have all shivered in our own isolation, and this book is also written with the hope that you, dear reader, might give it to someone who has caught a life chill, if only to remind them of the warmth of the giver and to find warmth therein.

I suspect that there are those who might find a book called "Dear Friend" a little corny or intellectually insubstantial. Too bad. Friendship doesn't require us to be smarter or cooler. Sometimes being too cool is living in a world that is too cold. Fashions have seasons. Friendship is always in season.

A friend is someone who allows you distance but is never far away. This is a book for friends near and far, new and dear. Friendship has gotten me through nights I never could have traveled alone. May some of the thoughts you are about to read also become your friends along the way, and as I say good-bye, let me say, "Hello, my friend."

Noah

"The only way to have
a friend is to be one."

—Ralph Waldo Emerson

Dear Friend...

*Thanks for the lesson
in self-esteem:
All friendship first begins
with self-friendship.*

Dear Friend...

Thanks for the medical lesson:
Friendship is contagious
and love is the contagion.

Dear Friend...

Thanks for the lesson on luck:
If we look at our friends
and feel lucky, we are.

Dear Friend...

Thanks for opening your heart.
When a friendship opens,
it opens us inside out.

Dear Friend...

Thanks for saying "Boo!"
It's scary when we think that
familiar fears are our friends.

Dear Friend...

*Thanks for teaching me not to
be blind to friendship even if
you sometimes have to close
one eye to make a friend and
two eyes to keep a friend.*

Dear Friend...

Thanks for lending me your keys.
Friendship is a key that can
unlock something inside of us
we never knew was locked.

Dear Friend...

Thanks for the medical advice.
Friendship is a lot like good health;
you don't know what you have
until it's gone.

Dear Friend...

*Thanks for reminding me that
a friend is someone who is there
for you when you don't think
you're getting anywhere.*

❧ ❧ ❧ ❧ ❧ ❧ ❧ ❧ ❧ ❧

Dear Friend...

*Thanks for all the time
we've spent together and for
showing me that friendship
can be our finest hour.*

❧ ❧ ❧ ❧ ❧ ❧ ❧ ❧ ❧ ❧

Dear Friend...

*Thanks for reminding me that
the only way to be a best friend
is to be the best I can be.*

Dear Friend...

Thanks for reminding me that who I once was is not as exciting to you as whom I might yet become.

Dear Friend...

Thanks for not laughing when
I looked ridiculous and not
ridiculing me when I couldn't
laugh at myself.

Dear Friend...

Thanks for reminding me that a clever character is not the same thing as someone with character.

Dear Friend...

Thank you.
Growing up, lots of people
would talk to me.
You would listen.

Dear Friend...

Thanks for listening long enough
for me to hear how wrong I could be.

Dear Friend...

Thanks for reminding me
that listening is sometimes
the most powerful thing
we can say to another.

Dear Friend...

*Thanks for being my friend
and reminding me that
things don't always go wrong
because we're wrong.*

Dear Friend...

*Thanks for reminding me
that it is all right to be wrong
and wrong to always be right.*

Dear Friend...

Thanks for reminding me that we offer others a chance to lighten their load when we say little and listen loudly.

Dear Friend...

Thanks for reminding me
that we can be independent
and still depend on others.

Dear Friend...

*Thanks for reminding me
that it is we who are lost
when we don't help others
to find their way.*

Dear Friend...

Thanks for reminding me that we learn a great deal about life and its burdens when we, by listening, quietly help others to unpack theirs.

Dear Friend...

Thanks for the arithmetic lesson:
In friendship the total is greater
than the sum of the parts.

Dear Friend...

Thanks for the lesson
in accounts payable:
Real kindness is helping someone
who can never repay you.

Dear Friend...

*Thanks for reminding me not
to take criticism to heart but to
get to the heart of the criticism.*

Dear Friend...

Thanks for reminding
me that all kindness
is not necessarily praise,
and all criticism is not
necessarily cruel.

Dear Friend...

Thanks for reminding me that anyone can show you how to peel an apple, but a friend is someone with whom you want to peel a moment— and taste its fruit forever.

❧ ❧ ❧ ❧ ❧ ❧ ❧ ❧ ❧ ❧

Dear Friend...

Thanks for the lesson in gift-wrapping:
No matter how gifted we are,
none of us are a gift to others if
we're wrapped up in ourselves.

❧ ❧ ❧ ❧ ❧ ❧ ❧ ❧ ❧ ❧

Dear Friend...

*Thanks for reminding me that
in friendship things can sometimes
get tough, and tough love can
sometimes be the thing that
keeps friends as friends.*

Dear Friend...

Thanks for encouraging me when times were tough and reminding me that good times don't always begin when things are great.

Dear Friend...

*Thanks for the encouragement
and for reminding me that
a ship that never leaves port
never discovers anything.*

Dear Friend...

*Thanks for reminding me
that we see friends every day
whom we don't recognize
simply because we haven't
met them yet.*

Dear Friend...

*Thanks for reminding me
that I'll always have problems
and remembering this might
solve a lot of my problems.*

Dear Friend...

*Thanks for not trying
to solve my problems but
reminding me that I could.*

Dear Friend...

Thanks for the cleaning lesson:
When you want to wash away
a bad memory, scrub with time.

Dear Friend...

Thanks for reminding me that
when times are tough and I feel
like I'm walking into the wind,
it might just be God exhaling—
and to take a deep breath.

Dear Friend...

Thanks for agreeing to run away and join the circus with me, but reminding me that even if we did this we'd still have to feed the elephants.

Dear Friend...

*Thanks for taking my side
in arguments and changing sides
when I changed my mind.*

Dear Friend...

❧

Thanks for waiting up for me,
and sitting up with me,
and putting up with me.

Dear Friend...

*You made a difference in my life
and that made all the difference.*

Dear Friend...

*Thanks for letting me sit
in the shade of your friendship
when things got hot.*

Dear Friend...

Thanks for reminding me that friendship is a club with admission restricted to members and nonmembers only.

Dear Friend...

*Thanks for having the honesty
to not accept my faults as yours.*

Dear Friend...

Thanks for the lesson
on the golden rule:
*A friend is more than someone who
treats us with the same familiar
disregard we have for ourselves.*

Dear Friend...

*Thanks for reminding me
that the opposite of love is
not hate but indifference.*

Dear Friend...

*Thanks for listening to what I said
and couldn't say, and understanding
that what we can't say hurts most.*

Dear Friend...

*Thank you for the lessons
on good, better, best:*

*A friend is someone who
brings out what is good in us.*

*And by this friendship invites
what is good to be better.*

*And in accepting the rest,
becomes a best friend.*

Dear Friend...

*Thank you for reminding me
that being a friend is the only way
to have one—and for being a friend
when I didn't know I had one.*

Dear Friend...

*Thank you for helping me up
when I stumbled over my faults
and for having the decency not
to mention what I had placed in my
own way—until I did it again.*

Dear Friend...

*Thank you for being a friend
to both my loneliness and
my need for aloneness.*

Dear Friend...

Thanks for everything you have given me, but thanks most of all for everything you have forgiven me.

Dear Friend...

Thanks for crying with me,
crying for me, and telling
me when it was time
to dry my tears.

Dear Friend...

*Thanks for making me laugh
when something happened to me
that was nothing to laugh at.*

Dear Friend...

Thanks for poking me
with your laughter when
I was full of hot air.

Dear Friend...

*Thanks for giving me
enough space to be
a close friend.*

Dear Friend...

Thanks for asking me
what I was going through
and reminding me that soon
I would be through it.

Dear Friend...

*Thanks for reminding me
that our friendship has less
to do with how important I am
and more to do with how
important I am to you.*

✽ ✽ ✽ ✽ ✽ ✽ ✽ ✽ ✽ ✽

Dear Friend...

*Thanks for reminding me
that love can demand less than
friendship because friendship
makes no demands.*

✽ ✽ ✽ ✽ ✽ ✽ ✽ ✽ ✽ ✽

Dear Friend...

Thanks for the balancing lesson:
A friendship requires both
an optimist and a pessimist.
And friends both think
each is the other.

Dear Friend...

*Thanks for compromising,
but never compromising
who you are.*

Dear Friend...

Thanks for reminding me that in friendship and charity it's less about giving and more about giving a damn.

Dear Friend...

Thanks for the monetary policy lesson:
In a friendship, the cost of saying
something negative is nothing against
the cost of missing the chance
to say something positive.

Dear Friend...

Thanks for accepting my faults and reminding me that any of us looking for a friend without faults won't have any friends.

Dear Friend...

Thanks for telling me of my strengths in public and my faults in private—and not telling me which you like more.

Dear Friend...

*Thanks for giving me
your smile to wear when tears
had washed mine away.*

Dear Friend...

Thanks for admiring my virtues
and accepting my vices even when
I wasn't capable of doing either.

Dear Friend...

*Thanks for reminding me
that a friend is someone
who allows you distance
but is never far away.*

Dear Friend...

Thanks for the lesson in flattery:
Do not confuse
flattery with friendship,
but be flattered
by your friendships.

❀ ❀ ❀ ❀ ❀ ❀ ❀ ❀ ❀ ❀

Dear Friend...

Thanks for the lesson in heroics:
A hero can be anyone who
turns an enemy into a friend
and never turns a friend away.

❀ ❀ ❀ ❀ ❀ ❀ ❀ ❀ ❀ ❀

Dear Friend...

Thanks for the lesson on family:
Friends are the family you choose.

Dear Friend...

Thanks for the lesson
in contradictory economics:
A friend costs nothing.
An enemy costs too much.

Dear Friend...

Thanks for the gardening lessons:
Friendship grows on you.
Friendship can blossom in any season.
Friendship can have dormant seasons.
Friendship is often a perennial.

Dear Friend...

Thanks for the art lesson:
Friendship is like a piece of art—
sometimes you have to step back
from a friend to get a closer look.
And when a friendship is a work of art,
it is a work in progress.

Dear Friend...

Thanks for the moving lesson:
Friends can move you to tears
and from tears to laughter.

Dear Friend...

Thanks for reminding me that a
good friendship is like a good wine:

It needs good grapes.
It needs time to mature.
And it drinks better if you
let it breathe a little.

Dear Friend...

*Thanks for the lesson
on finding the light:
Friendship is a reminder that
we are not alone in the dark.*

Dear Friend...

*Thanks for apologizing
when you were wrong and
for not reminding me
when you were right.*

Dear Friend...

Thanks for the lessons on values:
A friend is someone who values you.
What makes a friendship valuable
is not what you get from it
but what you give to it.

Dear Friend...

Thanks for reminding me
that friends don't take
a piece of your heart;
you give it to them.

Dear Friend...

Thanks for reminding me that our friendship is not only a gift to each other; it is also a gift from God.

Dear Friend...

*Thanks for reminding me to
use my stumbling blocks
as building blocks.*

Dear Friend...

*Thanks for reminding me
that the key to success is in
wanting less and utilizing more.*

Dear Friend...

Thanks for reminding me
to be cautious of living
my life in the past lane.

❀ ❀ ❀ ❀ ❀ ❀ ❀ ❀ ❀ ❀

Dear Friend...

*Thanks for reminding me
to be wary of thinking I can
buy what I hope to become.*

❀ ❀ ❀ ❀ ❀ ❀ ❀ ❀ ❀ ❀

Dear Friend...

Thanks for reminding me
to reach out to friends who
make me stretch.

Dear Friend...

Thanks for reminding me not to limit my aspirations to my desires.

Dear Friend...

Thanks for listening to me when I had nothing to say and for saying nothing about it.

Dear Friend...

Thanks for reminding me
that it's okay to strive
for what I want as long as
I also strive to be more
than what I want.

Dear Friend...

Thank you for reminding me that people who are busy bothering others are often the same people who have no time to bother about others.

Dear Friend...

Thanks for reminding me that
youth comes only once in a lifetime,
but there's no telling when it comes
nor how long it stays.

Dear Friend...

Thanks for reminding me that love is blind, but so is hatred, and to keep my eyes open.

Dear Friend...

Thanks for always being there.
Sometimes a friend even at a
distance can be your closest friend.

Dear Friend...

*Thanks for telling me
when I have something
stuck between my teeth,
even when it's my foot.*

Dear Friend...

Thanks for reminding me that
God gave me two eyes so I could see
both sides of my own opinions, and
two ears so I could hear both sides
to the argument, but only one
mouth and the reminder not to
talk out of both sides of it.

Dear Friend...

Thanks for reminding me that I'm not the most important person in the world but that you think the world of me.

About the Author

Noah benShea is a poet, philosopher, scholar, humorist, and international best-selling author. His books on Jacob the Baker are embraced around the world and have influenced generations. He has been an assistant dean at UCLA, and his work has been included in publications of Oxford University and the World Bible Society in Jerusalem. His weekly inspirational essay, "Noah's Window," has been carried nationally on the *New York Times* regional syndicate and was nominated for a Pulitzer Prize. Mr. benShea's recent award-winning book, *Remember This My Children*, was a finalist for the Gift Book of the Year. He is a frequent keynote lecturer who has spoken at the Library of Congress as well as to educators, businesses, and community leaders across North America. Widely interviewed on radio and television, Mr. benShea has two children, lives in Santa Barbara, California, and actually reads the mail at his website www.noahswindow.com.